Let's read and talk

Keeping Clean

Honor Head

W
FRANKLIN WATTS
LONDON • SYDNEY

Franklin Watts
338 Euston Road, London NW1 3BH

Franklin Watts Australia
Level 17/207 Kent St, Sydney, NSW 2000

This edition copyright © Franklin Watts 2014

Created by Taglines Creative Ltd: Jean Coppendale
and Honor Head
Author: Honor Head
Series designer: Hayley Cove
Editor: Jean Coppendale

Series literacy consultant: Kate Ruttle is a freelance literacy consultant and Literacy
Co-ordinator, Special Needs Co-ordinator and Deputy Head at a primary school in Suffolk.

All rights reserved.

ISBN: 978 1 4451 3212 9
Dewey classification: 613.4
A CIP catalogue for this book is available from the British Library.

Picture credits
t=top b=bottom l=left r=right
Cover images: frontr Natalya Bidyukova/Shutterstock; frontl maryloo/Shutterstock; back Rob
Marmion/Shutterstock
6 Andrey Stepanov/Shutterstock; 7t Sebastian Kaulitzki/Shutterstock; 7b Monkey Business
Images/Shutterstock; 8 Andrea Danti/Shutterstock; 9 Elena Elisseeva/Shutterstock; 10
Muellek Josef/Shutterstock; 11t Monkey Business Images/Shutterstock; 11b Mostovyi Sergii
Igorevich/Shutterstock; 12t StockConnection/SuperStock; 12b Natalya Bidyukova/
Shutterstock; 14 Jorge Salcedo/Shutterstock; 15t UltraOrto, S.A./Shutterstock; 15b aist1974/
Shutterstock; 16 Zsolt, Biczo/Shutterstock; 17l Kimberly Hall/Shutterstock; 17rt Arvind
Balaraman/Shutterstock; 18 Studio1One/Shutterstock; 19t Stepanov/Shutterstock; 19b Le
Do/Shutterstock; 20 Max Blain/Shutterstock; 21t Rob Marmion/Shutterstock; 21b Le Do/
Shutterstock; 22 Monkey Business Images/Shutterstock; 23l ZTS/Shutterstock; 23r
picturepartners/Shutterstock; 24 Dmitriy Shironosov/Shutterstock; 25t Tatiana Belova/
Shutterstock; 25b Sean Prior/Shutterstock; 26 Photononstop/SuperStock; 27 Cultura
Limited/SuperStock.

Printed in China

Franklin Watts is a division of Hachette Children's Books, an Hachette UK company.
www.hachette.co.uk

Contents

Pages marked with ⬇ have a free downloadable activity sheet at www.franklinwatts/downloads. Find out more on page 30.

Words in **bold** are in the glossary on page 29.

Why do I need to keep clean?

Keeping clean helps you to stay healthy and stops you from spreading germs.

What are germs?

Germs are tiny **organisms**, or living things, that may cause disease. They are so tiny you cannot see them. Many germs are infectious, which means they are passed from one person to another.

Being clean helps to keep germs away.

6

How do germs make us ill?

There are different types of germs such as **bacteria** and **viruses.** Some bacteria can give you **tooth decay** and a sore throat. Viruses give you illnesses, such as flu, mumps and measles.

This is what you may see if you look at germs through a **microscope.**

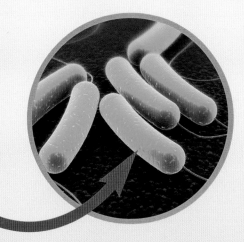

Talk about

✪ Why do you think it's important to stay clean?

✪ Where do you think you might pick up germs?

You are less likely to suffer from an illness caused by germs if you keep clean and fit.

Where do germs come from?

Germs are all around us. They are in the earth, in the air and in water. But if you keep clean and wash regularly you help to cut down the risk of catching germs.

How does my body keep germs out?

Your body is covered in skin, which helps to protect you from germs.

How does my skin protect me?

Your skin is made up of two layers: the **epidermis** and the **dermis**. Together they make a tough covering for your body.

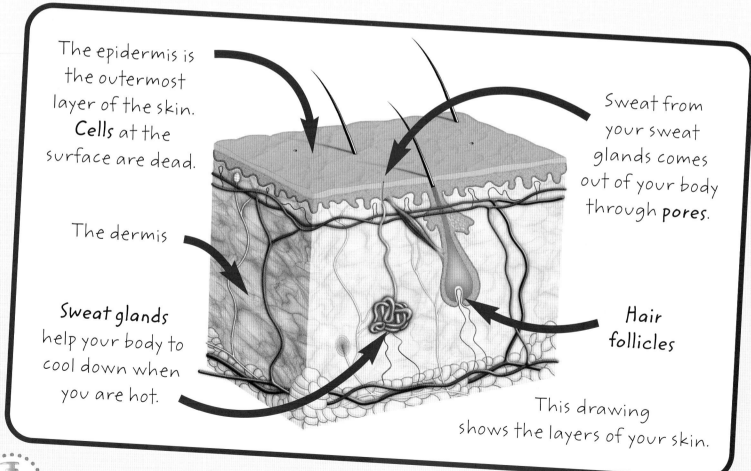

The epidermis is the outermost layer of the skin. **Cells** at the surface are dead.

The dermis

Sweat glands help your body to cool down when you are hot.

Sweat from your sweat glands comes out of your body through **pores**.

Hair follicles

This drawing shows the layers of your skin.

How do I keep my skin healthy?

Having a shower or bath and using soap helps to keep your skin clean and healthy. Eating lots of fruit and vegetables, and foods such as meat and fish are also good for your skin.

What else should I do?

Keep cuts and grazes clean. If germs get into a cut or scratch it may become **infected**. Make sure the wound is washed and keep it covered with a clean plaster or bandage.

You should cover a cut or graze with a plaster.

Talk about

- ✪ How often do you think you should wash?

- ✪ Why do you think a daily washing routine is important?

- ✪ Why might some people not bother to wash every day?

TAKE ACTION Write down every time you wash your hands in a day. Keep this list for page 28.

Why wash if I don't look dirty?

You need to wash to clean away sweat and dead skin cells that are on your skin even though you can't see them.

Does sweat make me smell?

When you get hot or do a lot of exercise you sweat. The sweat dries on your skin and your clothes. Sweat doesn't smell but bacteria grow in sweat and this may make a smell.

TAKE ACTION

Make sure you hang up your clothes when you take them off as this helps to air them and keep them fresh. It also helps to get rid of any dust they may have collected during the day.

Running around on a warm day can make you hot and sweaty.

Why do I have dead skin cells?

Your skin is made up of cells. Every day, millions of these cells die and are replaced by new cells. The dead cells rub off as you move about but most are trapped inside your clothes.

Washing clothes helps to keep them clean and fresh.

Talk about

- ✪ Why does it matter if someone is dirty?

- ✪ How does being clean make you feel?

How do I get rid of dead skin cells?

Having a wash, shower or bath gets rid of the dead cells. Also, make sure you wear clothes that are clean, especially underwear.

A wash in a warm, soapy bath helps to keep your skin clean.

What's the best way to keep clean?

Washing with soap and warm water is the best way to keep clean.

Using a flannel and warm soapy water helps to wash away any dirt.

What should I use to wash?
Use a flannel or sponge to soap your body because this helps to rub off any dirt. Use your flannel to wash your ears. Never put anything like cotton buds into your ears as they could damage them inside.

Why should I use a towel after washing, bathing or showering?

If you don't dry yourself properly after washing you could develop rashes and red itchy skin. You should take special care to dry between your toes and behind your ears.

A towel helps you to keep warm after a bath or shower.

Talk about

- Why do you think you need a proper wash, shower or bath once a day?

- Are there times when it's more important to wash, for example after sport or a swim?

TAKE ACTION

Change your towel when it gets dirty, about once a week. Dirty towels may have germs on them.

13

Read about

What about clean hands?

Washing your hands is one of the best ways to stop germs spreading.

Why should I wash my hands?
When you wash your hands you wash away germs. If you have dirty hands you will leave germs on the things you touch. The next person to touch the same things will pick up the germs.

When should I wash my hands?
Wash your hands after you've been in the garden, playing in the park or been to the loo. Remember to wash your hands before preparing or eating food.

When you wash your hands use lots of soap and rub your hands together well.

What about my nails?

Your nails get dirty during the day. In the evening before bed clean your nails using soap and a soft nailbrush. Don't bite your nails or the skin on your fingers. This makes them sore and can cause infection.

Never poke under your nails with sharp objects – use a nailbrush.

TAKE ACTION If you bite your nails, talk to an adult or go online to find out how you can stop.

Talk about

✪ Why do you think it's necessary to always wash your hands after going to the loo?

✪ When are the other times when you should wash your hands?

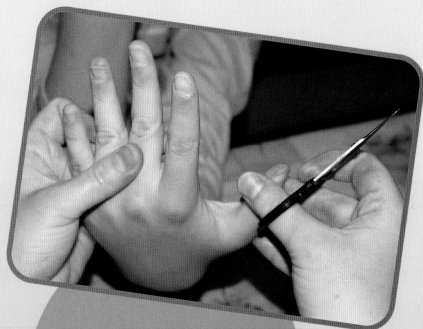

Keeping your nails short will help to keep them clean.

15

How can I stop spreading germs?

Follow some simple, healthy hygiene rules to help you stop spreading germs.

What if I have a cold?

It's very easy to spread germs through coughing and sneezing so take extra care if you have a cold. Always use a tissue to blow your nose, then throw the tissue away in a bin.

Cover your nose and mouth with a tissue when you sneeze or cough.

What other bad habits are there?

To see someone spitting is not nice for other people and spit is full of germs. Say no to nose-picking – keep a hanky or tissue handy for when you need it.

What about headphones?

Keep any headphones you use clean. Try not to share your headphones with anyone. If you do, wipe them with an **antibacterial** cloth before you use them.

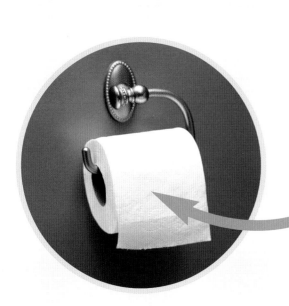

If you don't have a tissue to blow your nose, grab a piece of toilet paper instead.

You shouldn't share headphones, even with your best friends.

Talk about

⚙ Why is it important to stop germs spreading? What can you do to stop passing on germs?

Can I catch germs playing sport?

Germs are around us all the time but if you remember some basic hygiene rules you'll stay fit and healthy.

Does swimming keep you clean?

Swimming is a great way to have fun and exercise, but it's not a way of keeping clean. To get really clean you need to wash with soap and warm water.

Swimming is great exercise – but you still need to wash!

What about smelly feet?

Your feet sweat a lot when you run around and play games, especially if you are wearing thick sports socks and trainers. Bacteria grow in the sweat and this can make your feet extra smelly.

Wear trainers for sports but change out of them afterwards.

Talk about

⭐ Why are these good or bad things to do when you exercise – sharing towels in the showers, wearing swimming hats in the pool, wearing clean sports socks?

Put sports socks in the wash after you have worn them once.

Can you catch germs in changing rooms?

Most gyms and sport centres keep their changing rooms very clean. But because they are often warm, damp places, germs can grow there. Wash and dry your feet well after exercising.

Is clean hair important?

Keeping your hair clean makes it look and feel nice and keeps it in good condition.

Why does my hair get dirty?

Your hair grows from follicles in your skin. These follicles make oil to keep your hair smooth. This oil and dirt from the air makes your hair dirty.

How often should I wash my hair?

Usually your hair needs washing about twice a week. However, it depends on how long it is and how dirty it gets. It may need washing after an activity that has made you sweat a lot, and after swimming.

Wash your hair when it gets dirty or your head will start to feel itchy.

Is brushing good for my hair?

Yes, this helps to keep it clean and tangle-free. Use a wide-toothed comb to get rid of tangles. Wash your brushes, combs and scrunchies regularly.

Brush your hair gently to keep it looking good.

Wash your brushes and combs with shampoo.

Talk about

- How do you feel when you've just washed your hair?

- Why do you think it's important to keep combs and brushes clean?

21

How can I avoid getting head lice?

Head lice love hair and are easily passed from one person to another.

What are lice?

Lice are tiny, wingless insects that live by feeding on blood. Their eggs are called nits and they look like small white specks in your hair.

Why do lice love my hair?

For lice, your hair is a warm place where they can live and lay their eggs. Lice move from one person's head to another. They can live in any hair, whether it's clean or dirty.

Lice pass from person to person when their heads are close together.

22

How do I know if I've got lice?

If you have an itchy scalp or see small white specks in your hair, then you might have nits or head lice. Ask an adult to have a look for you. To get rid of lice you will have to wash your hair with a special shampoo. You will need to use a nit comb, as well.

A special nit comb will help you to get rid of nits.

To avoid spreading head lice, don't share your combs, brushes or hats.

Talk about

✪ What ways can you think of that head lice might spread from one person to another?

✪ How can you stop this from happening?

How do I look after my teeth?

For healthy teeth you should keep them clean and eat a good diet.

Why are clean teeth important?

Bacteria and other germs can collect in your mouth. They stick around your teeth to make **plaque**. This can cause tooth decay, which makes your teeth hurt. It may also make your breath smell.

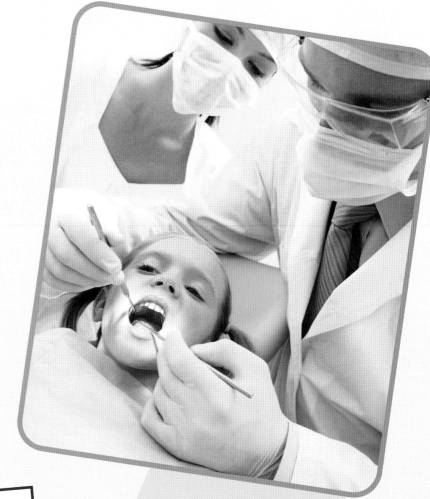

TAKE ACTION

Ask an adult to buy you a new toothbrush every three months.

If you get tooth decay you may have to go to the dentist more often.

How often should I clean my teeth?

Clean your teeth twice a day, in the morning and at night before you go to bed. You should brush your teeth for about two minutes each time.

What food is good for my teeth?

Lots of crunchy raw foods, such as carrots and celery, help to clean your teeth. Drink water rather than sugary, fizzy drinks. Fruit juice has **acid** in it, which can also cause tooth decay so don't drink too much.

Don't brush your teeth or gums too hard.

A salad with lots of crunchy vegetables helps to keep your teeth healthy.

Talk about

✪ If you had bad breath, would you want someone to tell you? What do you think is the best way to tell someone?

Why should I keep my room clean?

Keeping your room clean is healthier for you and is much nicer for your friends when they visit.

TAKE ACTION

Use a rubbish bin and empty it at least once a week.

Why is a clean room healthy?

Keeping old food, dirty clothes and used tissues lying around can spread germs. If you spill stuff on the bed or carpet, clean it up straight away.

What should this boy do to make his room clean and tidy?

How does my room get dusty?

When your skin **sheds** dead cells they lie around as dust. A lot of dust can cause **allergies** that make you sneeze, make your eyes itchy and can even make you feel sick.

Can my pets stay in my bedroom?

This is up to the adults of the house to decide. You don't have to shut pets out but remember they also leave hair and dead skin cells lying around.

If you have pets in your room it is even more important to keep it clean.

Talk about

- ✪ If you were visiting a friend, would you prefer their room to be clean and to smell nice?

- ✪ Why do you think adults always tell you to keep your room clean and tidy?

Talk about

✪ Check the list you made of the times when you washed your hands (see page 9). When did you wash them? Were there other times when you should have washed them? When?

✪ What should you do when you cough or sneeze to make sure you do not spread germs?

✪ Which of these pictures show you how to stop spreading germs?

✪ Why do you think it's important not to spread germs?

✪ If you see someone sneezing and not using a tissue, what do you think you should do?

✪ What words would you use to describe how you feel when you are clean?

Glossary

acid a substance that can slowly damage tooth enamel

allergies when certain foods or substances make you sick or feel unwell. For example, people with a pollen allergy sneeze a lot and may feel unwell in spring and early summer

antibacterial a substance that kills bacteria or germs

bacteria tiny living things that can cause disease

cells all living things are made up of millions of cells. Cells are so tiny they can only be seen under a microscope

dermis an inner layer of skin that contains blood vessels, nerves, oil and sweat glands

epidermis the name for the outer layer of the skin

hair follicles tiny tubes in the skin from which hair grows

hygiene ways to keep clean and healthy, such as washing your hands regularly to avoid spreading germs

infected when a cut is damaged further by bacteria

microscope an instrument used to see and study objects that are too small for you to see with your eyes

organisms tiny living things that can only be seen through a microscope

plaque a sticky material made up of bits of food, saliva and bacteria. Plaque collects around the gums, the edges of fillings and the surfaces of the teeth. Plaque contains acids that can damage the coating of the teeth and create holes or cavities

pores tiny holes in your skin

sheds loses or gets rid of something no longer needed such as dead skin

sweat glands curly tubes deep under your skin where salty water called sweat is made. The sweat travels up the tubes and out of tiny holes, called pores, in your skin

tooth decay when your teeth go bad and have holes in them

viruses tiny organisms (smaller than bacteria) that can cause diseases in plants, animals and humans

Index

Activity sheets

The following spreads have accompanying worksheets, which are available to download for free at www.franklinwatts.co.uk.

How does my body keep germs out? (pages 8-9)
A sheet that helps you find out how other animals keep clean and record your results in a table.

How do I look after my teeth? (pages 24-25)
Find out about the functions of different sorts of teeth and label the diagram.

Why should I keep my room clean? (pages 26-27)
Use this sheet to make a daily and weekly plan for keeping your home and bedroom clean and tidy.